ODE TO A BOY

Story By
Patty Ihm

Copyright© 2019 by Patty Ihm

All rights reserved.

Publisher's Note: This is a work of fiction. Names, characters, places, and incidents are a product of the author's imagination. Locales and public names are sometimes used for atmospheric purposes. Any resemblance to actual people, living or dead, or to businesses, companies, events, institutions, or locales is completely coincidental.

ISBN 978-1-947014-14-5

Printed in the United States of America

pattyihm.com
instagram: @pattyihm
facebook: patty.ihm

For My Boys

I know that the magic of those early years is part of who you are today, but still I miss you.

We sat together as you fell asleep on a lazy afternoon.

Your breathing slowed to a rhythm with mine.

The embrace turned to farewell as you left home, off to somewhere that would turn your childhood into a basket full of memories.

We watched the delivery man fill our dairy box so many times. There is a certain ethereal sound to the milk pouring from the glass bottle.

I know that when the days take you away from me, I will hear this sound of the milk escaping the glass, and I will share our memory of this wonder while I drink my coffee.

Though I prefer it black, I may take my coffee with a little bit of milk today, just so I can hear our sound.

Alone, I stand at the edge of the road.

The combine at the neighboring farm makes a *"whirr-clank"* sound as it moves through the late October days of harvest.

I saw you as a tiny boy, driving your cars along the edge of the kitchen table, and you were in the field next to me, tall as the corn.

Will you still go outside and look at the night sky with me when you come home from where your days have taken you?

Will the stars and the light of the moon still be enchanting and wonderful, as they once were when I held you on my hip?

Inside the diaper bag were animal crackers and your soft blanket.

Now there's a suitcase with a luggage tag that bears a different address, though your home will forever be here.

There is a rustle of leaves under my feet as I walk by myself through the woods on this sunny morning.

I had heard the same sound, and also that of your small voice as you called my name and pointed to the squirrel that you spotted on the trail, so many years ago.

In the stillness of the evening dark, we could hear the sound of an owl in the tree. I wonder, when you are having brave adventures of your own, if you ever think of me.

I found your tiny blue woolen mittens, the ones attached together by a string, when I was looking for mine today. I wished, for one more day, that if I pulled the string, your hand would meet mine at the other end.

The dance of the sun's reflection reminded me of you, as you would wiggle, perched atop the counter, while we kneaded the bread dough together. Today, as the familiar baking smell fills up the kitchen, I promise to save some rolls for you for the next time you find your way home.

I remember the first time I heard your deep, hearty belly laugh.

As we find ourselves at the harvest table, grateful for what we have, I can hear your laughter, and it fills my soul.

If I turned the doorknob ever so slowly and quietly, I could see you in your sleep.

I could watch the rise and fall of your chest; I almost knew your dreams.

Now, I hear the sound of the door, and I know you have come home.

I saw the sun today. It was fierce and bright, almost courageous in its stark beauty. It was just like you, my son.